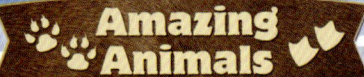

Narwhals

Addition

Logan Avery

Consultants

Colene Van Brunt
Math Coach
Hillsborough County Public Schools

Publishing Credits

Rachelle Cracchiolo, M.S.Ed., *Publisher*
Conni Medina, M.A.Ed., *Managing Editor*
Dona Herweck Rice, *Series Developer*
Emily R. Smith, M.A.Ed., *Series Developer*
Diana Kenney, M.A.Ed., NBCT, *Content Director*
June Kikuchi, *Content Director*
Susan Daddis, M.A.Ed., *Editor*
Karen Malaska, M.Ed., *Editor*
Kevin Panter, *Senior Graphic Designer*

Image Credits: front cover, p.1 Paul Nicklen/National Geographic Creative; pp.4–5 Dave Fleetham/Design Pics/Getty Images; p.6 (bottom) Paul Nicklen/National Geographic/Getty Images; p.9 WaterFrame/Alamy; pp.10–11, p.12 Flip Nicklin/Minden Pictures; pp.14–15 Nature Picture Library/Alamy; pp.16–17 Science Source/Getty Images; pp.18–19 National Geographic/Getty Images; p.23 Karyi Yeap/Shutterstock; all other images from iStock and/or Shutterstock.

Library of Congress Cataloging-in-Publication Data

Names: Avery, Logan, author.
Title: Narwhals / Logan Avery.
Description: Huntington Beach, CA : Teacher Created Materials, [2018] | Series: Amazing animals | Audience: K to grade 3. | Includes index. | Identifiers: LCCN 2017054938 (print) | LCCN 2018000917 (ebook) | ISBN 9781480759749 (eBook) | ISBN 9781425856809 (pbk.)
Subjects: LCSH: Narwhal--Juvenile literature. | Whales--Juvenile literature.
Classification: LCC QL737.C433 (ebook) | LCC QL737.C433 A94 2018 (print) | DDC 599.5/43--dc23
LC record available at https://lccn.loc.gov/2017054938

Teacher Created Materials

5301 Oceanus Drive
Huntington Beach, CA 92649-1030
www.tcmpub.com

ISBN 978-1-4258-5680-9
© 2019 Teacher Created Materials, Inc.
Printed by: 590835
Printed in: China

Table of Contents

Meet the Narwhal 4

Narwhal Facts 8

Magical Narwhals 18

Problem Solving 20

Glossary 22

Index 23

Answer Key 24

Meet the Narwhal

The sea is filled with **creatures**. Each one is **interesting**. Just look at the narwhal (NAHR-wahl).

A narwhal swims near the surface of the water.

Male narwhals have a long front tooth. The tooth looks like a horn. It is called a *tusk*.

Narwhals are called **unicorns** of the sea.

Only male narwhals have tusks.

LET'S DO MATH!

There are 8 narwhals swimming. Then 9 narwhals join them. How many narwhals are there now? Solve by drawing pictures or placing cubes on a part-part-whole model. Write an equation to show your thinking.

Whole ☐	
Part ☐	Part ☐

Narwhal Facts

Narwhals are whales. Each one is about the size of a minivan. These big whales spend most of their time swimming upside down!

A female narwhal swims in the ocean.

Narwhals live in the Arctic Ocean. They stay near the surface. They can dive deep below ice that forms.

These narwhals swim in a space between ice sheets.

It may be hard to spot narwhals. Narwhals can be blue, gray, or white. They are the same colors as ice.

Let's Do Math!

A **pod** of narwhals is swimming. There are 7 blue narwhals, 8 gray narwhals, and 3 white narwhals. Answer the questions.

1. Which groups of narwhals make a ten when added?

2. How many total narwhals are there? Show your thinking on an open number line.

Narwhals swim close together.

Narwhals live in groups called pods. They make sounds to talk to each other. These sounds include clicks, whistles, and squeaks.

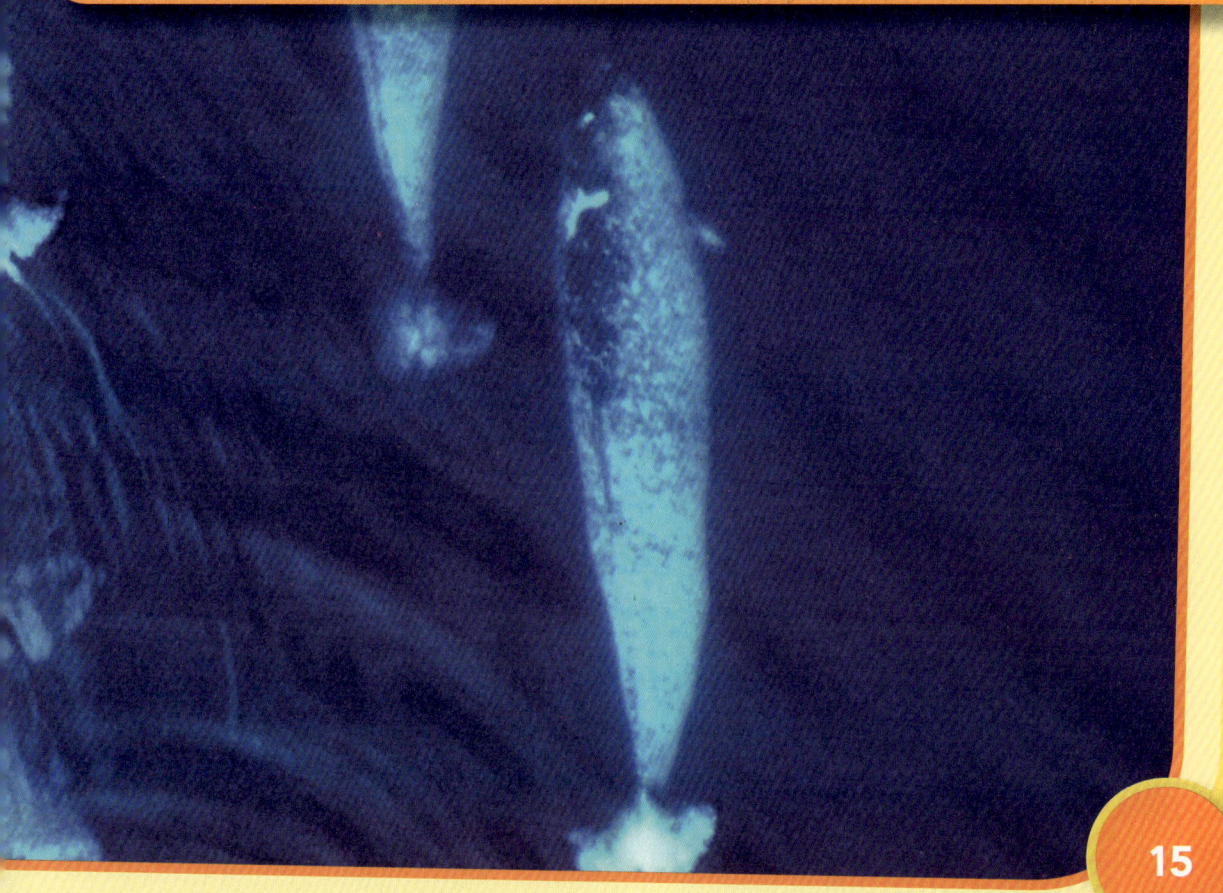

Narwhals are near the top of the **food chain**. They eat other sea creatures, such as fish, shrimp, and squid. But narwhals are food, too. **Orcas** and sharks eat them.

fish

shrimp

squid

LET'S DO MATH!

Narwhals are chasing sea creatures. There are 4 more squid than fish. There are 12 fish. How many squid are there?

1. Use the bar model to solve the problem.

fish	12	
squid		4

   ?

2. Which equation can help you solve the problem?

   A. $4 + \square = 12$

   B. $12 + 4 = \square$

Magical Narwhals

Narwhals are special. There are no animals like them. They almost seem magical!

Some narwhals gather to eat.

Problem Solving

A blue narwhal and a gray narwhal are eating sea creatures. Find out how many total sea creatures each narwhal eats. Then, answer the questions.

1. **a.** Does $4 + 7 + 6 = 4 + 6 + 7$? Why or why not?

   b. Does $2 + 8 + 5 = 5 + 8 + 2$? Why or why not?

2. How can making tens help you solve addition problems?

3. Which narwhal eats more sea creatures—the blue or the gray? How many more?

sea creatures	number of sea creatures eaten	
	blue narwhal	gray narwhal
squid	4	2
fish	7	8
shrimp	6	5
Total	☐	☐

Glossary

creatures—animals

food chain—series of living things that shows how one living thing uses the next living thing for food

interesting—not boring

orcas—a type of whale

pod—group of living things that live and travel together

unicorns—imaginary animals that look like horses with long horns on their foreheads

Index

Arctic Ocean, 10–11

colors, 12

food chain, 16

ice, 11–12

pod, 13

tooth, 6

whales, 8

Answer Key

Let's Do Math!

page 7:

17 narwhals;
8 + 9 = 17

page 13:

1. 7 and 3

2. 18 narwhals

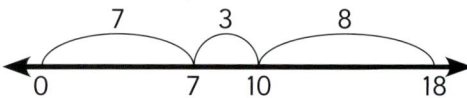

page 17:

1. 16 squid

2. B

Problem Solving

1. **a.** Yes; both equations have totals of 17.

   b. Yes; both equations have totals of 15.

2. It is easy to add numbers onto 10.

3. blue narwhal; 2 more